Well, Really!

Well, Really!

Lynda Mackenzie

Well Really

First Published in 2017 by FastPrint Publishing
Peterborough, England.

Copyright © Lynda Mackenzie, 2017

The moral right of Lynda Mackenzie to be identified as the author of this work has been asserted by her in accordance with the Copyright, Designs and Patents Act 1988 and any subsequent amendments thereto.

All rights reserved. No part of this book may be reproduced in any form by photocopying or any electronic or mechanical means, including information storage or retrieval systems, without permission in writing from both the copyright owner and the publisher of the book.

This novel is entirely a work of fiction. The names, characters and incidents portrayed in it are the work of the author's imagination. Any resemblance to actual persons, living or dead, events or localities, is entirely coincidental.

A CIP catalogue record for this book is available from the British Library

Paperback ISBN 978-178456-496-4

Printed and bound in England by
www.printondemand-worldwide.com

www.fast-print.net/bookshop

Introduction

Well, Really! is a light-hearted look at life from sixty-something; an age when your prejudices are fully honed, you have accepted that much of modern life leaves you completely bewildered but when all else fails you still have your sense of humour.

A series of monologues about a fictional family and friends, interspersed with rhymes, prose and the odd limerick.

"I have to say, George, that this afternoon, one hour of yoga had my body in positions beyond anything involved in the conception and birth of two children."

Cover sketch by Hamish Malcolm.

Proceeds to the Seagull Trust – www.seagulltrust.org.uk.

In memory of Ffodos.

A cat with too much personality

whose exploits inspired me to start writing.

Contents

page		
	1	Daffodils
	2	Introducing Emily
	4	The Last Straw
	6	At the Back of the Drawer
	7	Bonding
	10	The Birthday Party
	12	Tea and a Scone
	15	Over the Garden Fence
	17	Breakfast
	18	Exercise is Good for You
	21	What Have I Done?
	22	Economy Break
	24	Spring is Sprung
	27	The Cliché Police
	29	The Journey
	31	Lend a Hand
	33	A Letter of Complaint
	35	Let There Be Light
	38	Being Santa
	41	Limericks
	42	More Tea, Vicar?
	44	The Night Before Christmas
	46	The Big Day

48	Fantasy Dinner Party
50	Don't Go Into The Potting Shed!
52	Bedtime Story
54	The Picnic
55	The Party's Over
57	A Fitting Send-off
59	Cold Hands
61	The Times They Are A-changing
63	Missing
65	Going, Going, Gone
67	Small Talk
69	The Three Moons
71	Here Be Dragons
72	What's in a Name?
73	Snow
75	The Canal Festival
77	Little Weeds
80	That was Very Strange
82	The Five Senses of Christmas
84	A Dream Holiday in Limerick
86	Acknowledgements
88	About the Seagull Trust

Daffodils

Well really, George, that was beyond embarrassing! When Mrs Watson mentioned that she just happened to be looking out of her bedroom window and noticed our magnificent display of daffodils I had just begun to thank her for the compliment when you had to jump in and say that we didn't have any daffodils at the foot of our hedge and what she had seen was a magnificent display of dandelions. I tried to laugh it off but I'm sure she saw me glaring at you – her eyesight isn't that bad.

So, no trip to the coffee-shop for us this morning – we're going straight home so you can dispose of said dandelions, even if it takes you all day with or without recourse to a machete, flame thrower or explosives. I'll bring you regular cuppas to keep your strength up. Then we'll plant something else, horticulturally acceptable in the Avenue and any colour but yellow, so that Mrs Watson knows that whatever flowers she sees the next time she's hanging out of her bedroom window aren't daffodils or dandelions.

You know, George, now I come to think of it, I've never really liked daffodils – or Mrs Watson.

Introducing Emily

Emily, darling, be a good girl for Granny and unlock the door. There's a dear. Yes, you must be a big girl now if you managed to reach the lock. Grandad put it higher up after the last time we had this conversation. Now please, sweetheart, pull the bolt back and open the door. Granny would like to use the toilet.

Emily, why are you running around? Because I can hear you, dear, that's how I know. Oh, you're making pretty patterns on the floor. Er, what with, dear? With talcum powder! Oh. Well never mind that now. Just stretch up and unlock the door. But why can't you reach? You could reach up to lock it. You had your shoes on then. Well pop them back on now, please. Granny really needs to go to the toilet quite soon. No, Emily, Granny isn't "bursting for a pee." Wherever did you hear that expression? From Daddy – I might have known.

Come along now poppet. Put your shoes back on for Granny. Why can't you, Emily? But how did they get wet? Well putting them in the toilet isn't the usual way to clean shoes, darling. I'll tell you all about boot polish some other time, once the door is open and Granny's been to the toilet. Oh, Emily, please don't turn on the tap. That doesn't help me at all. Yes, it WILL wash all the toothpaste away. I'm trying to keep up, dear, but it's a bit difficult when my mind's on more basic matters. Now turn off the tap, thank you, and tell granny why you squeezed all the toothpaste into the washbasin in the first place. Yes, I do realise, now that you mention it, that I hadn't ever actually told you

NOT to squeeze toothpaste into the basin, but really, that isn't a valid reason to do it.

Now, Emily, let's get back to getting the door open. Granny's had an idea. Can you reach the towel on the back of the door? Yes, the big green one. Of course you're a clever girl to know all your colours. Now can you spread the towel on the floor? Yes, the floor is black, or black with a white pattern just at present. Right, sweetheart, fold the towel over and over so you can stand on it and reach the lock. Quickly, now, Granny's bladder isn't as robust as it used to be. That's it. Well done, Emily. Now, give Granny a quick hug then go downstairs while I go to the toilet. No, dear, I'll clean up the talcum powder later. DON'T TURN ON THE BATH TAPS! Oh, Emily, too late. Yes dear, you're quite right. Granny has had a little accident!

The Last Straw

George,

I just have time to write you a quick note while I'm waiting for the ambulance. I hope you enjoyed your golf with Roger today as it may well be your last for a while. Just after you left, Valerie appeared on the doorstep to ask if I would keep Boris for a couple of hours as she'd managed to get a last minute cancellation with her 'colourist' to get her roots done. (I don't know why she can't just have a hairdresser like lesser mortals do, but 'Gianetta' is apparently the best in the county – as if we don't know she was christened Janet!)

But anyway, off she went leaving that hound in my care with the information that he could be doing with a walk as he hadn't been out this morning. So Boris and I set off for the woods. Valerie had only left me the extending dog lead but I managed fine to begin with. I gently let him out and reeled him back in if I saw any other dogs. All went well until he caught sight of a squirrel. I retracted him immediately but pressed the button the teensiest bit too hard and he shot towards me through the air and landed in my arms. (I knew buying that white anorak in the Sale was a mistake).

Anyway, this must have damaged the lead's mechanism, because after the squirrel incident it would only extend, so by the time we got home I was trailing him by a good twenty feet. How we managed to avoid garrotting that child I'll never know, but I took Boris straight into the garden to keep the mud off the new carpet. I gathered up as much of the loose lead as I could and tied him to a fencepost with every knot in the Girl Guide Handbook (1964 edition) but the sneaky little blighter must have been sitting on some of the slack and I tripped over it, and my new glasses shot off into the petunias. Well really, that was the last straw! After scrabbling around to find them – mercifully undamaged – I turned to go inside for a very well earned cuppa, but the dratted Boris wanted to play and I somehow tripped over the lead again, hurting my wrist as I spread-eagled myself inelegantly on the decking. Hence the ambulance I'm waiting for. The emergency operator said my injury didn't sound urgent enough for them to 'blue light' me so I'm waiting patiently while Boris is attempting to dig his way in through the patio doors – for a Yorkshire Terrier he's very determined.

I tried to call Valerie but her phone's switched off. Apparently Gianetta insists on telecomm silence to allow her clients to 'fully enjoy the tinting experience', so I left her a text IN CAPITALS to let her know what had happened. So either she or Roger can collect Boris, whom I never want to see again. As I said, this may be your last golf with Roger for a while until I get over today's experiences. He and Valerie may be amongst our oldest friends but at the moment they're off my Christmas card list.

I can see my ambulance at the end of the road. They're taking me to the new hospital with its streamlined fast-track A&E department, so it'll probably be even longer than usual 'til I'm processed and fixed up. Just get Boris back where he belongs then head over to the hospital where I'll hopefully be ready for collection.

Thanks, love.

At the Back of the Drawer...

At the back of the drawer is a ball of fluff,
And lots of other useless stuff.
A pack of mints, past their sell-by date,
An ad for last year's summer fete,
An electric plug from days long gone,
Before everything came with one already on.
An elastic band, a reel of thread,
A battery that's distinctly dead,
A raffle ticket that didn't win
And should have gone straight in the bin.
Grand-dad's penknife, a piece of string,
A solitary curtain ring.
A stub of candle, "just in case"
A wedding favour trimmed with lace.
A key to the door of the last garden shed,
A propelling pencil, minus lead.
A safety pin and two Lego bricks,
A wristwatch that no longer ticks.
Three old pens, two paperclips,
A plastic fork for eating chips.
I've forgotten now what I was searching for,
But I didn't find it at the back of the drawer!

Bonding

Isn't this nice, David? So lucky that you were able to give me a lift today. It's seldom I get the chance to see you on your own, so it's nice to have six and a half hours to catch up and do some mother/son bonding. Yes, dear, I've just brought the one bag as you insisted, but my handbag doesn't count – that's cabin luggage. I don't see why you were so fussed – there's plenty of room in the boot. Now then, what shall we talk about first? Oh, all right, "I solemnly promise not to talk for the next 350 miles." It is your car after all. Okay, I'm shutting up – for now.

Well, that's the first hundred miles done, so I think I'm entitled to a sentence or two. As you're getting petrol at the next service station, I'll pop out for a take-away coffee. My caffeine levels are seriously depleted. No, for once I don't need the loo. I do resent it when you say you're glad you didn't inherit my bladder problems. Let me tell you that if it wasn't for giving birth to you, I wouldn't have my bladder problems either!

Yes, I'll be as quick as I can. I'll go and get my coffee while you fill up. Aargh! Don't you worry dear, it's nothing serious. Your mother just spread-eagled herself on the forecourt. I forgot that your car is about a foot higher than mine is. Yes, yes, I'm going for my coffee, just as soon as I've picked myself up.

Right then, off we go again. I'll just pop the sweeteners through the hole in the lid. Oops! Well really! How was I supposed to know it was powdered and not a tablet? You may say the mess doesn't matter, but I can tell by the look on your face – the spitting image of your Grandad – that the mess DOES matter. I'll try to clean up the powder and luckily most of the coffee spillage landed in my lap. The cup's very hot but that'll help keep me warm along with the damp trousers as you seem to like driving in Arctic temperatures. And by the time I've drunk it all it'll be about lunchtime. Okay, I'm shutting up again.

Is it alright to speak, now that we've stopped for lunch? Thank-you. You go and see what there is for lunch while I pop to the loo. What a wait! I politely held the door open for a lady with a walking frame and an entire coachload tailgated through behind her – every one of them headed for the Ladies. Right then – lunch. Oh, you've had yours. Well, thank you for that! I know you want to get back underway as soon as possible but I must have some form of sustenance. I'll nip into M & S and grab a salad to eat on the way. Yes, I really will be very quick – there's no queue.

Thank you for waiting, David. For a few moments there I wondered if you might drive off into the sunset without me. That was a joke, dear, not a serious option. I'll just munch my way through this mountain of lettuce in the hope of finding a tasty morsel hidden at the bottom. Oh, dear, how did that happen? Stop growling, dear, and don't grind your teeth. Quality dental work is very expensive. Lettuce is easily picked up. Now if you could drive extra steadily for a bit, I'll unfasten my seatbelt and get all the mess tidied. What's that beeping noise? Well my car doesn't get upset if my passenger takes the seatbelt off while we're moving, although, now I come to think of it, I don't have many passengers these days. Right, that's me all strapped in again and I'll stop talking for a while. Just remember that you're letting me off at Junction 3 for your brother to pick me up for the last bit of my journey. Yes, shutting up now.

Thank goodness we're here. I've tied up my rubbish in this carrier, so it's easier for you to pop in your bin. No, David, I can't take it with me and put it in Ross' bin. Why should I? I already have two things to carry while I wait. They'll make it awkward enough to have a coffee and get to the loo again. But just think, David, if this house hunting trip is successful we could soon be living only 40 minutes from you instead of being 350 miles away. Won't that be lovely? Oh, he's gone. I wonder if it was something I said?

The Birthday Party

Angela, dear, how nice to see you. Such a good idea, having a surprise party for Derek. And where is the Birthday Boy? Isn't he a bit old to sulk? Well I can understand that wearing a badge the size of a dinner plate proclaiming "I'm 70" isn't everybody's idea of fun, but it isn't your fault he didn't want his age known at the Golf Club. And anyway, 70 is the new 50, so somebody says. Don't try to work it out, dear; you know Maths was never your strong point.

Now what can I do to help? Shall I find more glasses? I see Colonel Brackett is swigging straight from a bottle. Where did you get the wine, dear? I don't recognise the label. Well, discount supermarkets did get good reviews in the "Which?" wine guide but I don't remember the Poundshop being included. But it's well chilled and alcohol's alcohol after all.

Angela, just how many people did you invite? And how many wine glasses do you have? So we're about a dozen short. It's your Maths again. Well, if you get those odd tumblers that everyone has at the back of their cupboard, I'll pop upstairs and add the tooth-mugs. Yes, I'll check your Auntie Vera hasn't put her teeth in it. It's such a strange habit she has – taking out her dentures whenever she visits the bathroom, but at least she's remembered to pull up her knickers today, even if she has tucked her skirt into them. Good thing everyone's used to her funny little ways.

I've sent George upstairs to try to persuade Derek to come and join his party. I must say it seems rather an over-reaction just because of the badge. Does he realise that at least half of the Golf Club is here? Well, shouldn't you have remembered he'd fallen out with most of them because of that habit he has of clearing his throat whenever someone starts taking a putt? Well, yes, if they're magnanimous enough to overlook it just today, he should be able to ignore their opinions of his driving style.

Oh, look, here he comes. Should we sing Happy Birthday? Looking at his expression, perhaps not. And he isn't wearing his badge. Right then, everyone, let's have a round of applause for our reluctant Birthday Boy. Oh, good, he's going to make a speech, he must be feeling better about the whole thing.

Well really, Angela, even with your Maths you should have been able to calculate that Derek's only 69 this year!

Tea and a Scone

Right then, Auntie, let's get on our way. Coat ready? Yes, this is a new coat I'm wearing. Do you like it? Well, technically, no, I didn't actually need a new coat, but it was in the sale and I liked the colour. And it was reduced by 40%. Yes, that does make it a better proposition. Now then, do you need to go to the toilet before we leave? Better to go, just in case. I'll just pop down to the office and sign you out. I'll meet you at the front door.

All settled, Auntie? Good. Well, I've told the office we'll be back about 4 in plenty time for your dinner. No, that really is plenty of time – trust me on this one. Yes, your hair looks fine and I'm sure most people don't realise it's a wig, particularly if you could break the habit of straightening it every time you pass a mirror. Yes, I can wait until you go to the toilet again, but use the one on this floor to save going back up to your room. Yes, they're all cleaned regularly and I'm sure no men use this one. Off you go – again.

Okay then, that's your walking frame in the boot – just. This car has a very small boot. Sorry, Auntie, but it isn't really practical for you to sit in the back. It's a 2 door car so you'd have to sort of reverse in through the space behind the front seat and I don't know if I'd be able to get you out again without the aid of a crow bar or the Fire Brigade. How about I push the front passenger seat back as far as it will go and then you'll have plenty of leg-room, it almost looks as if you're sitting in the back and I'll pretend to be your chauffeur? Although a 2 door pink Mini isn't the usual for a chauffeur driven limo! Yes, you have to wear your seatbelt – it's the law and we aren't going anywhere until you do belt up.

And we're off – at last. It's only a 10 minute drive to the Garden Centre where we're having tea. I really think you can hang on that long without going to the toilet. Now then, what news do I have since I saw you last? Oh, yes. Did you notice I've had my hair cut? Well, my ears haven't changed so it must be the style that makes them look as if they stick out. Thanks for that. Here we are then. I'll just extricate your walker from the boot and we'll negotiate the ramp. The toilets are over there on the right. I'll go and recce the scones in the meantime.

So, what will we have? The scones are plain, fruit, wholemeal or cheese and there are muffins too – choc chip, double choc chip, blueberry, coffee, coffee and walnut or cranberry. Perhaps you should have a cranberry muffin – cranberries are supposed to be beneficial for overactive waterworks. No, you just eat them, dear! Moving on, let's get a table and I'll go and get the teas. Have you decided what you want? A plain scone with butter, not margarine. No jam? Sorry, I'd forgotten about the problems a raspberry seed can cause with your dentures. There you are. A nice pot of tea. Yes, they warmed the pot and they're real tea leaves – no tea-bags here. Gosh, I'm ready for this. It's been a long afternoon.

Well that was a lovely cuppa, Auntie, wasn't it, but we'd better start getting you home in time for your dinner. Again? Well, it must be almost half an hour. I'll wait by the door.

And that's you home again. I'll see you up to your room. Remember you were going to give me the remains of that box of chocolates with all the ones you don't like. Are you sure they're all too hard for your teeth? The descriptions on the box don't always indicate how hard they are. Well, I suppose it was sensible of you to try them all to make sure so I'll be sure to look out for teeth marks! Thanks, Auntie. I'll just be off now before you pop to the toilet again. It's been a lovely afternoon. I'll see you again in a couple of weeks. Bye for now.

Over the Garden Fence

This is the tale of Hall versus Spence,
And tells of the feud over their garden fence.
The fence in question was made of chain-link,
And quite inoffensive or so you would think.
When the Spences moved in, they thought it too bare –
Their plan was to plant a new shrubbery there.
But the previous owners, a family named Scott,
Had been friends with the Halls and they'd chatted a lot
As they leaned on the fence, discussing the world.
In order to do this, access was required.
And hoping for similar friendship, chez Spence,
The Halls were desirous of keeping the fence.
They wanted the Spences to just leave it as is –
No plants near the fence – all were in quite a tizz.
The Spences hit back by planting at night.
Gardening by moonlight – now that was a sight.
Then the Spences went off for a month in a villa
And the Halls were revenged with the aid of weed-killer.
Dead foliage galore then greeted the Spences,
Who were coming to dread any mention of fences.
But they didn't give up – success at all cost,
So woven rush matting was nailed to each post.

That lasted a week until a bonfire
"Accidentally" torched it. They were back to the wire.
The introduction of moles to disturb the foundations
Did nothing at all for the neighbours' relations.
By now, all were exhausted – a break overdue,
So the Halls headed off for two weeks in Corfu.
They no longer wished to be friends with next door
The whole business had shaken them both to the core.
Inspired in their absence, Mr Spence made a call
To arrange for a builder to fashion a wall.
It was splendid and solid and six feet in height,
A quite undisputedly magnificent sight.
The Spences relaxed, the fence was no more.
A small price to pay to even the score.
But what of the Halls, when home they flew?
Did they shout? Did they scream? Did they faint? Did they sue?
They were both quite delighted and dancing with glee,
They'd got what they'd hoped for – a new wall, for free!

Breakfast

Emily, dear, be a good girl for Granny and sit up at the table while I get breakfast. I bought a mixed pack of mini cereals so you can choose which you want while I put the kettle on and get the plates ready.

What's that dear? Mummy says mass produced cereal products are full of salt and sugar with more nutrition in the cardboard box than the contents. Really? That's interesting sweetheart. How about a slice of toast?

Well, no, actually it isn't home baked from organic, stoneground, unbleached multi-grained flour with New Zealand Manuka honey. I was thinking more along the lines of a slice of Warburton's Toastie with Golden Shred. Grandad has yoghurt in the fridge. Do you like yoghurt?

Sorry, poppet, we can't run to unsweetened Greek with organic fresh fruit compote at this time of the morning. Grandad is happy with a strawberry Ski. But we do have free range eggs! How do you usually have your eggs?

Let me tell you, Emily, that in your house it isn't only the eggs that are coddled! Oh, look at this. What a pity you can't read big words until next term, like you told me last night. This cereal pack says it's made from organic brown rice with fair trade 80% cocoa butter chocolate and naturally occurring unrefined sugars. That's just perfect. Mummy will approve, I'm sure. Enjoy your Chocki-chunks, dear. Granny needs a shot of caffeine.

Exercise is Good for You

George dear, pop the kettle on, would you. I'm exhausted and desperate for some caffeine. What a day I've had! You know Sue had promised me a surprise for my birthday? Well, you'll never guess what she came up with. Nothing as commonplace as coffee 'n' cakes. Oh no, not our Sue. Sit down George or you'll fall down when you hear where I've been. Ready? Yes, okay, I'm getting there – just building the dramatic tension. I, George, have been to a GYM! Yes, a real live gym; short for gymnasium, from the Greek gymnos for naked. Oh no, George, of course I kept my clothes on. The world is far from ready for even the thought of my acres of naked flesh. No, Sue took me to her Yoga class – she thought it would relax me!

For a while I had no idea where we were going. We fetched up in the retail park. Oh good, I thought – cream tea in the garden centre. But she produced this enormous gift wrapped cylinder, ribbon bows and all. So I'm now the proud owner of a turquoise yoga mat. She led me into this sparkling new building – all chrome and light oak with 'musak' piped into every corner, even the loos. I suspect the perky receptionist had never before signed in someone with matching handbag and mid-heel court shoes. Luckily I was wearing my stretchy trousers (in anticipation of that cream tea) so they at least allowed for the possibility of movement.

The room we went into had mirrors all the way around – I saw views of my anatomy hitherto unsuspected. Sue directed me to position my new mat where I'd have a good clear view of the instructor. She then issued me with

2 purple foam bricks and a length of webbing. Well, yoga's one thing but a communal bondage session seemed a bit much for a Wednesday afternoon.

I looked around and there were bodies of every shape and size, but all very toned. I felt a bit lumpy but was still prepared to go along with the experience. Yards of lycra seemed to be holding everyone else's lumps in check, except for one lady whose DD cups were making a determined bid for freedom. You really couldn't tell if they were in trying to get out, or out trying to get in.

Then the lights were dimmed and the class began. We started by just lying flat, breathing deeply with the occasional stretch. I thought to myself, this is a doddle, and I can do this, but the lights went up again and we were off. Well, George, in forty years I've never had any reason to criticise your sexual inventiveness but I have to say that in one hour of yoga this afternoon my body has been in positions beyond anything involved in the conception and birth of two children! I've been a cat and a dog, balanced (not very successfully) on one leg, stretched in numerous directions and had my spine articulated. I didn't use the bricks, having decided by that time to 'rest' and watch the others and no mention was made of the webbing so I'll just have to let my imagination take care of that – perhaps I should have brought it home? We finished with 10 minutes of relaxation which was surprisingly enjoyable – I only just managed not to drop off. All in all, it could have been much worse. At least I didn't meet anyone I knew, although most of the people I know consider any form of exercise completely unpalatable.

And speaking of things unpalatable, Sue suggested lunch on the way out but I took one look at the mountains of lettuce and other overly healthy offerings on display in the cafeteria and dragged her in the direction of the garden centre where we had a sumptuous cream tea – at last. I'd just embarked on my third meringue when Sue popped to the loo, so I googled 'what to do with a turquoise yoga mat (slightly used)' and discovered they're apparently excellent for lining a cistern to stop condensation in winter, so the day wasn't a complete waste.

Now let's have that cuppa then I'll decide between a bungee jump and a sky dive for Sue's birthday next month.

What have I done?

What have I done? Just let me think,
I've scoured the oven and cleaned the sink.
I'm working my way through a very long list
Of household chores frequently missed.
I've been in the corners and under the bed.
I'd rather do anything else instead.
The cushions are plumped, the dog has been banished,
And all of my junk has temporarily vanished.
There really is so much to do –
Like polish the silver and clean the loo.
I've dusted the bookcase and vacuumed the cat
While it was lying on the kitchen mat.
So much to do and hide away,
Before my Mother-in-law comes to stay.

Economy Break

(or you get what you pay for)

Hello, Margaret, I simply must tell you all about our holiday. It was quite extraordinary – we've never experienced anything quite like it. It was one of those late availability internet deals – you know the kind of thing – 2 people, 2 nights dinner, bed and breakfast for a ridiculously low £80. Well, George flung himself wholeheartedly into seeing just how cheaply we could do it and you know what he's like in that kind of mood. He thought it would be 'fun' to travel by coach and so much cheaper. He found something called a Super Saver Senior Citizen Double Discount and it only cost £8 per person each way.

Well, I can now proudly declare I've been in every Service Station on the entire length of the M6. Every 30 miles or so, someone needed to use the toilets and the one on the coach was out of order, hence the need to visit all the Service areas. It made the journey seem twice as long but I must admit the M6 is one of Britain's prettier motorways. As we got farther north the scenery became quite spectacular and we were only 3 hours late in arriving!

Unfortunately, the Station Hotel where we were staying is next to the railway station, not the bus station, so we had to walk a mile and a quarter in a light drizzle – great for the complexion though. But, moving on, the hotel was lovely. I can really recommend it. Our room had a delightful view over the B&Q car park. George, of course, had to ask if any other rooms were available but they could only offer us one overlooking and downwind of the fish quay which started work at 4am. We declined.

After a lovely dinner I enquired about evening entertainment and we were directed to sit by the window in the lounge and just after 10 o'clock it started. All the local youths congregate in the square in front of the hotel and it's just a matter of time before the Police are called. The receptionist said you could almost set your watch by them. The Police always get there between 10.36 and 10.49. The kitchen staff place bets on each evening's arrival time. It was really a most entertaining and educational evening.

The next morning we set off on a day trip on the ferry to one of the nearby islands. It was a bit chilly but I managed to find a seat near the back with a nice warm draught from the kitchen extractor fans. So I had a good view from a nice warm seat with the added bonus of the aroma of frying bacon. Perfect.

That evening I had a bit of a mishap with my complimentary wine, but the waitress assured me they were quite used to mopping up spills and not to worry that it had lifted the polish from the table top.

So, after two nights, it was back on the coach for the return trip via the southbound service areas – a quite different selection of toilets. I really must recommend the trip to you, Margaret, although, if you can afford it, perhaps it would be worth upgrading the wine!

Spring is Sprung

Right then, George, let's get this new mattress bought. I can't say I'm impressed with the look of that sales assistant – altogether too perky and over made up, but we'll just have to hope appearances are deceptive. I bet she has some silly modern made up name.

Good morning. How good of you to interrupt your phone-call to serve us – and after just ten minutes. Now what's your name, dear? I can't quite focus on your badge from here. Ki-ora – oh, that's very retro and it matches the shade of your tan too. Now then, we need a new mattress. What do you have? Yes, I noticed that your 'sale' is in its last few days. Just as well as the posters are so faded they'll probably fall down on their own soon. Just before we go any further, can you uplift our old mattress? Well, I quite appreciate that you don't want to put anything dirty in your nice clean van, but I do think you could work on a more diplomatic way of conveying that. But never mind, onward to the beds.

You want us to do what, dear? Lie down on this electronic bed to 'assess our sleeping posture and comfort requirements'. Okay, but we'll feel a bit self- conscious lying on a bed in a shop window. You don't have any curtains or even a blind. We'll just have to hope no-one we know passes by.

Right, George, take off your shoes and your anorak – we need this to have at least a semblance of our normal bedtime routine. Well really, George, there's no need to take out your teeth. We're not being that accurate. Yes, Ki-ora, this is my usual sleeping position. Oh, I see, that screen shows the points of most pressure on the mattress. Red means too much pressure and the firmness needs adjusted. Gosh, my rear is showing as an enormous red block. Don't giggle, dear, you may well be this size one day. Right, so you adjust it until there are more yellow blocks than red ones. That's better; my rear is much less conspicuous. Now, how about the other side? George, there's something digging into the mattress and causing a red splodge below your waist? Well take your keys out of your pocket. You don't wear them in bed and they're giving false readings on the comfortometer. Quick George, lie down again. Mrs Arbuthnott is coming out of the shop opposite. I don't know which is the more embarrassing – you and I lying on a bed in a shop window or her being seen patronising a Poundshop.

Right then, Ki-ora, according to the machine, we need a medium-firm mattress. I suspect we could probably have arrived at that conclusion by non-electronic means, but let's move on to actually choosing a mattress. Gosh, it's very complicated. Open coil springs, pocket springs, memory foam, latex with memory foam, and that's before we get to 'toppers' which seem to have moved on from being hats. There are microfiber toppers, memory foam toppers, gel toppers. This is just too much for my ageing brain to take in, but I do know I don't want a memory foam one as the dips stay there all the time. Call me old fashioned – did you say something, dear, or were you just clearing your throat? As I was saying, call me old fashioned but I like my bed to look pretty during the day with a nicely laundered duvet cover and accessories. Tell me, do you have such a thing as a plain, straightforward sprung mattress, standard double bed size? Excellent. We'll have a quick bounce to make sure it's okay and settle on that one, I'm more than ready for a coffee. It's a pity the new one is so much deeper than the one we have. I'll need to buy new fitted sheets, but it can't be helped. They're all very deep, even minus a topper. No, dear, we don't want a special offer matching headboard. Why on earth would you want to match your headboard to you mattress?

Right then, Ki-ora, we got there in the end. Let's do the deal. HOW MUCH? I hadn't realised how out of touch we are with 21st century prices. What's that dear? You'll give me a complimentary fitted sheet as mine won't fit? Isn't that a nice gesture, George? You know, as soon as we came into the shop didn't I say to you that Ki-ora looked a complete sweetheart!

The Cliché Police

It was a dark and stormy night and the cliché police were on patrol. They had explored every avenue and would leave no stone unturned to ensure those who lived their lives surrounded by comforting clichés would have the full weight of the law brought to bear upon them.

It was raining cats and dogs. Inspector Calls and his trusty sidekick, Sergeant Major were soaked to the skin as they lurked in the bushes, waiting for their suspects to put in an appearance. They had successfully apprehended two wrongdoers in this exact spot just last week and a little bird had told them history would repeat itself tonight and two more unimaginative conversationalists would be caught in the act.

Mavis and Doris had been having the time of their lives at bingo, each winning the princely sum of £20. They were now wending their way homewards deep in conversation about their nearest and dearest.

'Well,' said Mavis, 'You know what they say – there's no smoke without fire. And remember where he comes from – like father, like son.'

'Yes,' replied Doris, 'what goes around comes around. They'll just have to grin and bear it, but there'll be tears before bedtime, you mark my words.'

Inspector Calls pounced. 'Gotcha,' he exclaimed, 'Mavis Muirhead, I'm arresting you and your partner in crime, Doris Douglas, for speaking in non-stop clichés. You do not have to say anything but anything you do say will be taken down and may be used in evidence against you.'

Doris mumbled 'knickers' under her breath, but Mavis was more philosophical.

'It's a fair cop,' she said, 'You done me bang to rights, guv. Slap on the bracelets, I'll come quietly.'

'Yes,' said Sergeant Major, 'Your chickens have come home to roost!'

The Journey

Right then, Emily, into the car and I'll fasten your seatbelt, then we'll be off. It's been lovely having you to stay but Granny isn't as young as she used to be and I must admit I'm rather tired, but we'll have you home in under an hour and I'll be back in time for Bargain Hunt. No, Emily, Granny doesn't 'have the hots' for Tim Wonnacott. I just happen to appreciate a smartly dressed man in a bow-tie.

And we're off! Yes, dear, I packed your anorak and yes, I can see the gatepost. It was really a very small scrape last time and Grandad might never have noticed it if you hadn't told him!

Yes, I see the red light and I'll be sure to stop at the crossing. And yes, I can see that it's turned green now but it isn't really acceptable to drive off while there's someone still on the crossing – particularly someone with a pushchair, and yes, I packed your anorak.

Right then, that's us clear of the town. Now, what shall we count to pass the time? Red cars or sheep? Pubs! But why, Emily? Because Mummy and Daddy always count pubs on this road and go into the third one – The Old Goat – and Daddy always laughs and says he's exchanged one old goat for another. Oh that's hilarious Emily. Not! Let's just listen to the radio. It won't be long 'til you're home and yes, I packed your anorak.

Emily, stop making those rude gestures out the window. That Policeman looks rather annoyed. No, dear, he isn't pulling us over just to say hello. Good morning, officer. Yes,

I realise my Grand-daughter was sticking out her tongue and making rude gestures, but she is safely belted in and I'll make sure she's belted up as well from now on. Thank you for being so understanding.

Well really, Emily, that was embarrassing. Being stopped by the Police on the dual-carriageway. Now let's just get on our way again and for the last time, yes, I packed your anorak! Why do you keep asking me? Well if you saw it hanging in the hallway as I locked the front door why didn't you say that? Oh, Emily. No Bargain Hunt for me today. I wonder if that Policeman would notice if I did an illegal U-turn?

Lend a Hand

Joyce, look at that man on the old fashioned shop bike with the big basket at the front. Doesn't that take you back? I have to say he's going a bit fast considering he's in a public park. And now he's waving at everyone. Well really. He's going faster and faster and I can hear his brakes squealing – perhaps he can't stop. Oh dear, he's going to crash. I can't watch. You'll have to tell me what happens – I've closed my eyes. Come on, Joyce, what's going on? I can hear screams. You're no help at all, I'll have to look for myself. Oh, my goodness, he's lying in a tangled heap amongst those hydrangeas. Poor man. We'll have to go over and try to help, although, yet again, I suspect our 1960s Brownie First Aid badges aren't going to be of much use. Not too quickly though and with any luck someone better qualified than us will get there first. Look, Margaret's there, thank goodness. It's safe to approach now, she'll know what to do – her husband's a vet.

Can we do anything, Margaret? The poor man seems very agitated. Paltry? I don't think having your leg lying at an unnatural angle can be described as paltry, dear. Oh, poultry! He had hens in the basket and they've escaped. Of course Joyce and I will round them up. Only too pleased to help. Come along, Joyce. We're looking for two brown hens and one black that cost more than the other two put together, hence the reason he's so upset about them.

Now then, where have they got to? Look – there's the black one perched beside that waste bin; I'll grab it while you ferret about in the undergrowth and try to get the other two. I can see something moving amongst those berberis bushes. Off you go. No, I can't help, I'm wearing my new slacks and berberis is notoriously jaggy – people used to plant it to deter paperboys from taking short-cuts across their lawns. Whatever happened to paperboys? Gone the way of milk bottles and a second postal delivery, probably, but moving on, I happen to know you bought that skirt in the millennium sale at McNab's in the High Street, so it's more than old enough that it's no loss to your wardrobe if it gets snagged. Gracious, look at the time, stop scrabbling around and come out of there at once, Joyce. Let's get this fowl back to Margaret and head home or we'll miss the beginning of Countdown.

What an exciting afternoon that was and it just goes to show that it's right what they say – a bird in the hand is worth two in the bush!

A Letter of Complaint

Re Amazon Kindle

Dear Amazon,

I am writing to complain about the above product which I received as a birthday gift from my son. As the packaging gave no hint of the purpose of the product, I initially thought it was a device to help me light my fire. Having shredded the said packaging and placed it among the coals and wood, I then endeavoured to produce a spark of some kind from said Kindle. This was spectacularly unsuccessful.

I then carefully re-assembled the packaging in the hope of finding some clue as to the real purpose of the item. This led me to the term "e-reader". I was little the wiser, and almost immediately discarded the idea of an online opticians chart as that would surely have required more than one letter on it to fulfil its requirements.

Help came in the guise of Mavis next door's grandson who informed me behind what can only be called a smirk that I could buy books to read on my Kindle. I just needed to set it up on my computer. Now I know you are sitting there, somewhere up the Brazilian jungle laughing at me, but I do have a computer – what do you think I'm using to write this if not my faithful 1994 desk-top. My family rue the day they introduced me to e-mail, although I do try not to bother each of them more than five times a day.

Young Jasper informed me I had credit of £25 which I could spend with just a click. Splendid. I immediately downloaded Fifty Shades of Grey and am looking forward to 1-clicking my way through the two sequels, once the Doctor has my blood pressure back under control.

So, basically, my complaint is only with the name of the device. If I made these mistakes, surely others will do likewise, especially as I understand you have another, similar product called a Kindle Fire! I feel it would be to your advantage to address the matters mentioned in this letter – do not underestimate the value of the (fifty shades of) 'grey pound'.

Yours sincerely,

Let there be Light

Is that you, George? Well, yes, I suppose it is unlikely that anyone else would unlock the door and shout 'I'm home'. How was the golf today? You only lost three balls? Well done – that's a real improvement. Well, while you were off enjoying yourself I've had a most traumatic afternoon and the most annoying aspect of it is that I cannot find any way to blame you for it; but don't worry, I'm working on it.

It all began when I was on my way home from lunch with Joyce and I remembered that the bulb in the lamp on the landing died last night and we'd used the last spare one a couple of weeks ago. Why is it that when one lightbulb blows, others always seem to join in? Do you think they're all in a union or something? Anyway, I thought I'd just pop into the DIY store and get a replacement. Now, the last time we were there the lightbulbs were right at the back of the store in the farthest corner from the entrance, but when I got there I was confronted by a huge display of loft ladders and one of those irritating smiley faces on a board telling me that the lightbulbs were now in aisle 42 upstairs. Of course, the stairs are back near the entrance, but I'm sure the exercise was good for me.

Having located aisle 42 – back in the far corner again – I was confronted by an entire aisle of lightbulbs of every shape and size. When did they become so complicated? I approached the oldest assistant I could see but he couldn't have been more than 19 and asked him where I would find a 60watt lightbulb. He informed me in what must be described as a somewhat condescending manner that bulbs were no longer made in watts – they were now in lumens, but I could get a 60watt equivalent. Of course, I have absolutely no idea what a lumen is, although, in fairness I'm not too sure exactly what a watt is either, but I do know what a watt does and I know we need 60 of them to light the landing. My juvenile tutor patiently explained to me that there were approximately 10 lumens to a watt so I needed about 600 lumens.

Fair enough – I could cope with that, but next he mentioned GLS. I informed him that in my day they were GCEs and what did that have to do with lightbulbs? George, did you know that old fashioned bulb shaped bulbs are called GLS? Don't fib, dear, of course you didn't. Anyway, I said I needed a pointy one and his level of superiority upped a notch as he told me they were candle bulbs. Well, really. There were also shelves of what I call ping pong balls which are apparently properly described as golf balls – but not a dimple in sight so I reckon they've got that wrong. I remembered from the last time the landing lamp needed a bulb that a ping pong ball wouldn't fit as the skirt thing that keeps the shade on the lamp is too deep for them to fit, hence the reason we need candle shaped ones. I'm not completely stupid, you know!

So, having ascertained that I required a 600ish lumen candle bulb, my helper and I then delved into the realms of bayonet fittings and Edison screws. No, George, I hadn't heard of them either, but I now know that screw in bulbs can be Edison screw or small Edison screw, whereas the old fashioned push down and turn ones can be bayonet or small bayonet. An un-necessary complication comes in the fact that SES or SBC stand for small screw or small bayonet. I helpfully pointed out to the lad that the S could just as easily mean standard. I could see him taking regular deep breaths by now, but we were on the home straight. All that remained to be decided was whether I wanted a clear or opaque finish. I was almost past caring but remembered that the clear ones cast rather harsh shadows so I opted for opaque.

Eventually, I bought a pack of four but I've kept the receipt, just in case. I suspect I've become an anecdote for the lad to share with his mates. And you know, George, now I come to think of it, it was your fault, after all. When you used the last spare bulb, you should have immediately gone into 'head of the household hunter gatherer mode' and set off at once for the DIY store to hunt and gather a pack of 625 lumen opaque BC candle bulbs and spared me all this hassle. Well really.

Being Santa

Hello, Joyce, thanks for getting my coffee. Whatever are you drinking? Well, it may be called festive red berry tea with cinnamon stick and orange segment, but it looks like weak Ribena with a twig in it. I don't see any orange – well if they've run out of orange you should have complained and threatened them with the Trade Descriptions Act. How does it taste? Like weak Ribena with a twig in it – I rest my case. I hope it doesn't stain your teeth – Isabel had a real problem with cheap red wine, but she was able to get the stains off by soaking her plate overnight in biological washing powder and bleach. She thought she'd rinsed it thoroughly but when her husband saw her the next morning he started humming 'I'm for Ever Blowing Bubbles'.

Anyway, sorry I'm a bit late. George is in the middle of the mother and father of all sulks – it's into its second week. He maintains it's all my fault and I reluctantly have to agree with him, for once. It all began when I met Christine a few weeks ago and she was bemoaning the fact that the Senior Ladies Bridge Club was having a problem finding someone to play Santa at their Christmas 'do'. The butcher from Castle Street has done it for ages but he isn't available this year as he's been tagged after that stalking incident and has to abide by his curfew. She asked if George might be willing to help out and I didn't see why not. He wasn't best pleased when I told him, but reluctantly agreed.

Things began to go a bit wrong when we opened the box with his outfit and found that the top on the tube of glue for the beard was completely stuck. There was no time to get a new tube so I just smeared on some Evostick – three years past its sell-by date – and managed to get the beard in place. I dropped him off as he found it a bit awkward to drive in Wellies and long cloak and agreed to collect him at 10 o'clock.

When I did get him home the tale he told was really quite incredible. I still suspect it wasn't as bad as he says – you know what he's like, I've told him a million times not to exaggerate. Anyway, according to George by the time he was ready to start handing out the gifts, a considerable quantity of alcohol had been consumed by all – they were drinking Pimms from pint glasses. He'd expected that as each lady's name was called he'd approach her and hand over a modest gift. But what actually happened was that he was ensconced in a throne-like chair and the ladies came to him and climbed on to his lap for a cuddle! Poor George was embarrassed beyond belief as they began to tickle his beard and snuggle into his lap. Although by this time the Evostick was beginning to react with his skin, so he said he was almost glad when someone tickled his beard as it helped ease the itch. He had to endure these antics about twenty times, each lady trying to outdo the previous one with her level of coyness and originality of her wriggling!

When he dared to make a comment to Christine about their behaviour, she just put on her best 'head-mistress' look and said that the butcher had never objected. Of course, he was always what we used to call 'a ladies man' even before his wife passed on. Oh no, dear, his wife isn't dead – she just passed on to the fishmonger and became a born again piscatarian. Apparently she can't look at a lamb chop now without fainting.

Anyway, George managed to survive the repeated onslaught of the entire Ladies Bridge Club but by the time I arrived to collect him he had resorted to hiding in the Gents and would only unlock the door when I proved who I was by whispering his mother's maiden name as a password. Even then, we had to run the gauntlet of the more forward club members who formed a guard of honour between the Gents and the door. Instead of crossed swords they all pulled up their sequined skirts to expose a line of lycra encased thighs. By this time even I was feeling a bit queasy and wishing we were home.

And the night's traumas were not yet over. We still had to remove the beard. I googled 'remove a beard stuck on with Evostick' but we didn't have any of the suggested solvents, but continued applications of white spirit, surgical spirit and nail polish remover finally loosened it enough for me to ease it off. But his face is still very red and blotchy and he hasn't been able to shave since. So, of course, every time he looks in the mirror he remembers what happens and revs up his sulk level again. I really need some suggestions on how to get him back to normal. I've already promised he need never set eyes on any of the ladies again, although I suspect they might well be more embarrassed by their behaviour than George was – I hope they would be. What a wonderful idea, Joyce. Why couldn't I have thought of that. I'll pop straight into the chemist for a large economy sized bottle of soothing balm for 'mature men's skin'. Perfect. Thanks so much, Joyce. See you next week. Bye.

Limericks

An accident prone lad, named Chuck
Was in need of a good bit of luck.
Trying to rescue his dog,
He'd stepped into a bog
And was completely and utterly stuck.

Young Archie who lived in Athlone
Made a date with a lass, name of Joan.
But Joan preferred Clive,
So failed to arrive,
And poor Archie was left on his own.

A spinster librarian from Fife
Often wished she could relive her life.
She'd spend less time on books
And more on her looks
And this time, might end up a wife.

A poem will often be lyrical,
A formula may be empirical,
But to write a good rhyme
In a short space of time,
Now that really would be a miracle.

More Tea, Vicar?

Hello, Sue, have you heard? Yes, it's all true. My sister-in-law's cousin, Jean, lives next door to him and she's seen it for herself. She's been keeping an eye on him since he moved in, just to see how housetrained he is for a single man. She says he changes his bed regularly if not frequently, so that could be worse, but she wanted to know what he was hanging on the little washing line in the corner and she just happened to be standing on the water butt last Monday when she saw them – yes, four pairs of what were most definitely ladies underwear! Beautiful pastel colours, high cut legs and cream lace trim. A bit scratchy I would have thought, but never mind that. Jean's positive there haven't been any lady visitors since he moved in and she would have been sure to see them arrive now she's installed CCTV in her driveway and binned her nets.

Look, he's just come in. Teapot at the ready, Sue. Well really, he's been annexed by Iris. She's on the hunt for husband number five – but she doesn't know what we know – yet. She's talked him into a slice of her Victoria Sponge – he'll regret that. It'll lie in a lump in his stomach for hours.

But back to the underwear. Jean checked later in the week for nighties or tights but there were just more pants, so I suppose that's something. She can't check any more since she fell through the lid of the water butt. Luckily it's been dry recently – just her slippers she ruined. Of course, anyone with any sense would have worn wellies, just in case.

Here he comes again, ready for a top-up to help Iris's sponge go down. You really wouldn't know to look at him, would you? Not even a Visible Panty Line!

Hello there. More tea, knicker – I mean Vicar?

The Night Before Christmas

Come along now, Emily, let's get these toys tidied. It's Christmas Eve and Santa won't deliver to an untidy house. Ouch! Why is it that Lego is so painful when you stand on it, even through a slipper? We must clear plenty space for that bike you asked him for in August. He was probably still on his holidays but hopefully he left the AdminElf in charge.

Emily – what's wrong, sweetheart? Why are you crying? Well of course you don't need two bikes but why would you think Santa would bring two? Oh. Well maybe what you saw in the garage wasn't a Barbie-pink bike with streamers on the handlebars. It could have been any number of things. I know – it was Daddy's bike with the box of Christmas decorations balanced on top with tinsel falling over the edge. I'm sure that's what it was. Really. Now, don't worry.

Grandad and I really enjoyed your Nativity Play last week. Yes, I know you were disappointed not to be an angel, but you made a very pretty cow. Of course everyone knew it was you under the mask. We could hardly avoid knowing after Dexter the sheep from next door shouted 'Emily's a cow' when you made your entrance. Tell me, dear, why were there only two wise men? Well, I must say Mrs Jackson should have known better than to wash velvet at 60 degrees. It was bound to shrink. Couldn't they have found a smaller king to wear it? Mid-calf length robes would have been quite acceptable. Jason was the smallest available? Okay. But I can quite see why he was so embarrassed that he felt the need to lock himself in the toilet rather than expose his knees to public gaze. And it was very enterprising of the second king to explain his absence by saying that Tesco had run out of Myrrh so he'd tried Asda instead and was currently trying to work out how to get through the self-service checkout. We could all sympathise with that!

Mummy's finished in the kitchen now. Last time I looked in she was stuffing mince pies into the turkey like there was no tomorrow. When Grandad and Daddy disappeared off to the pub she positively growled and attacked a pile of sprouts rather viciously. But she's gone off for a nice relaxing bath now. I'm sure she'll feel better after a candle-lit soak and a glass of wine. She took the bottle in, did she? Oh, dear, I didn't realise things were that bad.

Now then, Emily, I hope you're going to be a good girl tomorrow morning and stay in bed until a reasonable hour. Grandad and I love coming to stay with you at Christmas but being woken at 4.30 last year was a bit much. Who said Grandad gets grumpy? Well, I'm quite sure I never said it out loud. But anyway, now that you've learned your alphabet and how to tell the time, you'll be able to understand this year that Santa delivers alphabetically so won't get to Scotland until at least 7am.

Right then, that's the tidying done. I'll pop up and check Mummy's still sober and hasn't drowned then I'll text Grandad to say it's safe to come home as all the work's done. Then it's off to bed for you and we'll all be ready for the experience that Christmas Day is sure to be. Yes, we'll put out a mince pie for Santa and carrots for Rudolph. It was very thoughtful of you to forego your carrots at tea time so that Rudolph could have them. Right then, Emily, off to bed and we'll see you in the morning – but not too early or not just Grandad will be grumpy. Night, night and Merry Christmas, Emily!

The Big Day

Ne'er cast a cloot 'til May is oot
My Mother used to say,
So she wanted me to wear a vest
Upon my wedding day.
She found a lacy one for me,
White, of course, and frilly,
But I'd set my heart on a strapless gown
Wouldn't that have looked just silly.
She next suggested a cardigan
In case I caught a chill.
She made me one in double knit
With pockets and a frill.
Worn down, I agreed to a high necked frock
Once worn by Great Aunt Anne.
Mum was delighted, she'd got her own way,
But I had a cunning plan.
The bridesmaids promised not to tell
Just what I had in mind,
And Dad just didn't notice
But then a Father's love is blind.
So when Mum set off for the church,
Having checked I was wrapped up warm

I quickly binned the dingy frock,
And shrugged off the inevitable storm.
And so I floated down the aisle
Bare shouldered in satin and lace
And a lasting memory of my Wedding Day
Is the look on my Mother's face!

Fantasy Dinner Party

Your Royal Highness, how nice to meet you. Do come in. Yes, I would appreciate it if you could help me up – that curtsey was a bit deeper than I had planned. Now if you could take my arm to steady me, I'll just climb up the coat-stand and get vertical again. That's better. Yes, I know two of the hooks are loose – it's on George's 'to do' list. Now, this is an informal gathering so may I call you Anne? Certainly, Ma'am, of course I realise there's a protocol to be observed even on occasions such as this.

Most of the other guests have already arrived. You'll find Andy Murray and Rory McIlroy in the garden. I gave each of them a machete and suggested they practice their respective shots in the bramble patch at the far end. With any luck they'll have it all cleared by the time dinner's ready. I had hoped Bear Grylls would join them to make sure they came to no harm and found their way safely back to the house, but he swung off through the trees with a Tarzan roar, shouting something about catching dinner in the woods. He mustn't like the idea of my multi-buy M&S 'dine in with wine' offers.

Clare Balding is on the decking with binoculars, watching their progress and giving a commentary. Oh no, dear, it's not a nautical deck. The only water feature we have is a solar powered faux stone wishing well and windmill combo. Our deck is just a lot of planks laid to cover the bit of the garden nearest the house. Yes, I suppose it is somewhat of a bizarre concept when you put it like that. Well, off you go and talk horses with Clare. Perhaps you can put a stop to her unending piece to a non-existent camera. If you'll excuse me, I can hear another car outside. I expect that will be Dame Judi Dench.

Dame Judi, how wonderful of you come. Forgive me for not curtseying but I don't think the coat-stand would take the strain. Oh, I couldn't possibly call you by your first name, your Dameship – that would be much too familiar. But do come in – Clare Balding and the Princess Royal are talking horses on the er, deck, while Rory McIlroy and Andy Murray are playing explorers in what's left of the bramble patch. I'm just waiting for Bear Grylls to get back from wherever he swung off to – hopefully minus anything furred or feathered – and we can sit down to eat and discuss some of the really important matters of the day. Like who's going to win Strictly this year!

Don't Go Into The Potting Shed!

Don't go into the potting shed, Auntie. We've been round most of the garden so let's just sit on the patio and have a cup of tea and a biscuit. It's a beautiful afternoon. Such a shame your Care Home has no garden and I believe access to the balcony is banned since Mr Walker abseiled down his bed sheets wearing only a flowery shower curtain and see through boxer shorts. According to Mrs Elliot, who was either lucky or unlucky enough to witness the event, he bore a strong resemblance to a chicken in a roast-a-bag, complete with giblets.

Have a second cup of tea, Aunt Muriel. Aren't those pink flowers at the foot of the garden pretty? I'm not sure what they are but George calls them shit-so-stylus. I suspect that's not how it should be pronounced but saying it like that is the nearest he's going to get to swearing in my presence. When George gets home he'll give you a tour of his veg plot. It's his pride and joy. Where are you going? No, dear, our toilet's indoors. I really think it would be better if you used that and avoided the potting shed.

I hear a car – that must be him back. From the look on your face, George, I probably shouldn't ask, but how was the golf today? Well, golf balls are relatively cheap and it was probably wise not to go paddling in the pond to hunt for the four you lost. Those silly little golf towels aren't designed for drying your size tens! Do take Aunt Muriel round your veg plot. She's desperate to see your marrows. Yes, I've warned her not to go into the potting shed but she seems strangely attracted to it. Off you go and I'll pop into the kitchen and make a fresh pot of tea.

Right then, that's the kettle boiled. I can just see George and Aunt Muriel up to their knees in over-sized marrows. Oh dear, George has become entangled in the support string and she's off towards the potting shed again. Why does it fascinate her so much. Oh, my goodness! What an appalling scream! Poor Auntie. I told her not to go into the potting shed!

Bedtime Story

Right then, Emily, off you go to bed and I'll be up in five minutes to read you a story. What's that, dear? Well, I don't know about making one up – what's wrong with all the stories in your books? Oh well, of course if your other Granny can make up stories I'm sure I can too. Make that ten minutes instead of five – I'll need to get my imagination in gear.

So, are you all snuggled up? Who's the current cuddly friend? Still Teddy or has Peppa Pig returned from the big bacon factory in the sky? Panda? Well you and Panda can cuddle up while I tell you all about a little dog. His name? Does he need a name? Okay then. Once upon a time there was… because it's my story, Emily, and I want my story to begin with once upon a time. Now where was I?

Once upon a time there was a little dog called… Brian, who was bored with playing in his garden. He'd had enough of digging holes in the borders and chasing his ball. No, dear, dogs can't really skip or play on swings or on trampolines, that's just for little girls or boys. Anyway, one day Brian was digging at the foot of the hedge when he found a small hole that was just big enough for him to squeeze through. Don't fidget, dear. Lie still and remember you're supposed to be going to sleep.

So when Brian emerged on the other side of the hedge he found himself in a great big field, and standing in the middle of this field was a very big goat! Brian had never seen a goat before – what's that, dear? If he'd never seen a goat before, how did he know it was a goat? Fair point.

Will you PLEASE keep still. What's wrong with you? Oh! Off you go then and quickly. You really should have remembered to go before you got into bed – we don't want any accidents.

Right then, Emily, back under the covers. Unfortunately you missed the most exciting part of my story while you were at the toilet but I'll continue now that you're back. Panda can tell you all about the bits you missed. He really enjoyed it. So Brian was very glad to be safely home in his own garden. He ran into the house, gave himself a good shake to get rid of all the bits of mud and grass then snuggled up in his bed and went to sleep just like you're going to do, so we can all live happily ever after. Good girl. Night, night, Emily.

The Picnic

Because the sun was shining
Because the sky was blue
Because they were on holiday
Because a picnic was something to do
Because they must have sandwiches
Because they fancied "old fashioned pop"
Because neither of these were in the house
Because they needed to shop
Because they couldn't start their day
Until they dealt with each delay
Until they reached the picnic ground
Until a better spot was found
Until the flies were kept at bay
Until the blue skies turned to grey
Until the rain came pouring down
Until each smile became a frown
Until picnic dreams were put away
Until the next year's holiday

The Party's Over

Bye then, Jim, and thanks very much. It was a super New Year party. Sorry, Rosemary, I refuse to do even one more 'air kiss'. My lips have been permanently puckered since midnight. When did we stop just shaking hands at New Year? I blame the EU, so maybe now that we're Brexiting we'll stop pretending to kiss each other and get back to good old fashioned limp hand-shakes. Anyway, I'll give you a ring in a couple of days. No problem, we were glad to help with the clean-up, weren't we, George? Bye, then.

Right, George, let's get off home. Do stop muttering. It's not far, just along the Avenue then down the hill. Shouldn't take much more than ten minutes. Gosh, the fresh air is making me a bit light-headed. Who would have thought that after a lifetime of refusing alcohol because I didn't like the taste, I would have finally found something I loved. Pity it's Champagne though – a bit expensive for your average, everyday crisis. I had decided to be abstim…, abstem…, abstum…, not to drink too much tonight but Rosemary and I found a nearly full bottle when we were wiping down the worktops and it seemed a shame to waste it. I only drink once a year too, or should that be twice a year, once before midnight and once after, which is a new year? Oh, my head.

I think I'd better take your arm, George. George? Where are you? Well really, George. Couldn't you have waited until you got home? Or you could have gone before we went. And on Mrs Thompson's prized camellia too. I know camellias like acid soil but that's ridiculous. I can only hope she blames that Great Dane from the house next to the Post Office. I don't know how his wife puts up with those strange foreign habits of his. Come on now, there's a group of revellers on the other side of the road. 'Hello there, Happy New Year to you too.'

Right then, round the corner and it's not far down the hill. Oh dear, we seem to be veering from side to side and I'm sure we're gathering speed. Let me just grab this lamp-post and we'll stop here a moment and make a plan. My head's getting fuzzier by the minute. I hate to think what I'll feel like in the morning. I had planned on getting up early to watch the New Year's Day concert from Vienna but that's not going to happen. I have the Radetzky March going on inside my skull already. At least the BBC has stopped showing the Edinburgh Tattoo on New Year's morning. That was really painful.

So, are we ready to deal with the rest of the hill? I reckon if we aim diagonally across towards just above the gate into No 17 and bounce off their hedge then back across to No 20, avoiding the holly bush, a final diagonal should land us directly in our drive. Gosh, who would have thought that Champagne could improve one's grasp of geometry? Or do I mean Algebra? Anyway, let's get going.

Oh, what a relief to be home. I have my key all ready but I can't seem to locate the keyhole. George, I think you'd be better at this, and quickly, dear, if you can, as my bladder has reached its maximum capacity. Thanks, George. Happy New Year.

A Fitting Send-off

Well, George, I must say that was lovely. Don't look at me in that tone of voice – it is perfectly acceptable to refer to a funeral as 'lovely'. It's not as if I said it was 'wonderful' or 'beautiful' or even the much over-used 'amazing'. It was a lovely send-off for Lily. A good turnout too. Quite a respectable number and no-one that was obviously just there for the tea and scones afterwards. Were the scones nice? I didn't have one. I didn't want to risk my new crown on an over-baked crust.

Nice choice of music too, although I found the coffin coming in to 'Sheep May Safely Graze' a bit odd as Lily absolutely hated anything to do with nature. Even a visit to the Botanical Gardens was too pastoral for her. I think it came from living most of her life on the 19th floor of her tower block. Not even a view of a tree without benefit of binoculars. She once tried growing runner beans of all things on her balcony but they 'ran' up to the 20th floor and her upstairs neighbours harvested any beans that survived the altitude.

I suppose there had to be family flowers and they were very pretty but I don't know who chose lilies. I can see why they did, with her name being Lily, but she hated lilies even more than other flowers. Something about pollen from the lilies in her bouquet staining her dress at her first wedding and she thought it was a bad omen. Well she got that right. It didn't last above 18 months.

On that subject, I thought the celebrant – is that the right word? – glossed nicely over her two previous marriages, but if that was supposed to be a joke about Jim being her toy boy it didn't go down too well, although technically correct as he's only 89 and Lily was 96.

I heard someone say Lily suggested the committal music herself – she wanted something from her younger days, going to the dancing during the war. Such a shame they played the wrong track on the CD. Gracie Fields was very apt but 'Wish me Luck as you Wave me Goodbye' caused a few sharp intakes of breath and a couple of giggles surfaced too.

All in all, a nice service, although I did think it was a bit off for the celebrant – is that the right word? – to hand out her business cards to everyone who looked over 75. Did you keep the one she gave you? I didn't get one, of course.

Yes, it was a lovely funeral.

Cold Hands

Nigel sat in his favourite chair and perused the morning paper. He felt a rush of cold air on the back of his neck. Before he could even turn to see its source two cold hands grasped his neck.

'It's freezing today,' said the owner of the hands. His wife, Hilda, drew her thickest cardigan around her thin frame and moved to turn up the radiator. Nigel sighed and removed his sweater.

'I'm just popping out to the shed for a bit, dear. I won't be long.' As he retreated, he considered Hilda's apparent inability to EVER be the correct temperature. She could go from too hot to too cold in minutes, summer or winter. She'd always been that way but it did seem to be getting worse as she grew older. For her age, Hilda was remarkably healthy, but you wouldn't know that to listen to her. Her imagined illnesses were legendary. It could be said that she 'enjoyed poor health'.

Hilda never caught a cold. Oh, no. In the manner of the Queen Mum, Hilda caught a chill. These chills very often morphed into the latest strain of influenza which then, of course, threatened to develop into pneumonia. The medical dictionary she'd found in a charity shop had been confiscated by Nigel after the expected tiredness that followed a day's gardening had been translated into chronic fatigue syndrome and a slipped disc. Every headache had the potential to be a brain tumour. Any abdominal pain was the forerunner of appendicitis or some type of stones.

Gall stones, kidney stones, Hilda knew more about stones than the local builder's merchants!

After a happy hour, pottering in his shed, Nigel returned to the house to find all the windows wide open and the radiators turned off. He put his discarded sweater back on and went into the kitchen where he found Hilda – stripped down to her vest.

'Oh, dear,' he thought, 'here we go again,' wondering whether a faulty thermostat was a recognised medical condition. Hilda was seated at the kitchen table, examining her right foot with the aid of a magnifying glass.

'Look at this,' she invited. 'I'm sure I have gout.'

'Oh, Hilda,' he said in exasperation. 'You're such a hypochondriac.'

'That's as maybe,' sniffed Hilda, 'but I'm a sick hypochondriac.'

The Times They Are A-changing

Sunday October 30th

Well, George, today's been a fiasco and a half! And it was all your fault. Yes, I know everything always seems to end up as your fault, but this time it's true – it all began when you forgot to change the clocks back in March. I couldn't have been expected to remember – I was having one of my heads. Such a shame we were an hour late and missed little Horatio's christening, but the one we did see was very nice – a little girl christened Petunia and you don't get many of those nowadays!

George, wake up dear, I'm talking at you. You can have a nap when I've finished. Anyway, I was so obsessed with getting it right this time that I made a careful list of all the household items which required changing. (Please note at this point, George, that the cooker was deliberately omitted from the list. I'll get to that later.) Now I WILL take responsibility for not allocating the items between us, but it was just an unfortunate accident that led to most of the clocks being put back twice, once by each of us. I did enjoy those two hours extra sleep though.

That on its own would have been bad enough – we'd probably have discovered our error when we switched on the TV or radio – but it was quite a shock when Bob and Helen arrived for lunch at what we thought was 11am, was really noon, but was what they thought was 2pm as they had put their clocks forward by mistake. We were all so confused but we synchronised watches and prepared to start the day again.

So with my planned lunch still frozen solid and the oven refusing to heat up because 'someone' had altered the auto timer – I told you I'd come back to the cooker – there was really no option but a nice walk followed by lunch in the pub. A nice meal, though, and after a few glasses of wine we all began to see the funny side of things.

We really must take more care to get it right next spring. In the meantime I'm off to hunt for the instruction book for the cooker or we'll have no hot food until we're back on BST. Right, George, you can now have your nap, but if I don't reappear from the cupboard in an hour, send a search party.

Missing

Emily, sweetheart, what's the matter? Why are you crying? You've lost your babies? Oh dear. When did you last see your dollies? Oh, not dollies – babies. Silly Granny. Well let's have a hunt for them, shall we? Where did you see them last? In the kitchen just before Mummy went out – right then, that's where we'll start. Are we looking for big dolls – sorry babies – or small ones? Of course, Emily, Granny should have known that all babies are small.

What's that? You like green babies best. I really can't get my head round modern toys; green dolls – whatever next? And there's a black baby too? I'm not sure if that's politically correct just at present, but moving on, there's no sign of any babies lying around in here. Where should we look next?

Well, I really can't imagine why they'd be in the fridge or the oven but I'll open them so you can have a look for yourself. Gracious – this oven hasn't had a visit from Mr Muscle for a while, but never mind that now, we're not here to criticise your Mother's housekeeping, or lack of!

No babies in the oven or fridge, Emily. Where do you suggest we try now? In the high cupboards? Surely not, dear. Please don't start crying again. Of course we'll look there if that's what you want. No babies in this one, just plates and bowls. On to the next one. What a lot of wine glasses your Mummy has. Oh, that's for when her friends come round every Tuesday for a Wine 'n' Whine. Gosh, what a lot I'm learning this morning! On Tuesdays you go to bed early and Daddy goes to the Tasty Tipple for the evening. Mmm. Perhaps we should move on to the next cupboard. I'll lift you so you can see if there's any sign of your babies? You've found them? Excellent.

Can you reach to get them out? Let me see, darling – oh Emily, they're Jelly Babies! I thought your Mummy was a sugar free eco-mother at the moment? Oh, that was before Daddy said naughty words and used her Modern Yummy Mummyhood magazine to light the barbecue. I see. Well perhaps you could have just one jelly baby before lunch. Yes, you can have a green one. Oh, Emily, you've eaten her head first! How could you!

Going, Going, Gone.

Good evening, Ladies and Gentlemen, and welcome to the annual charity auction at Gavel & Block Auctioneers. We have a varied selection of lots for you today, all kindly donated by local residents and businesses, so please bid with generosity.

And our first item is Afternoon Cream Tea for 4 at the Hilltop Luxury Hotel. Who'll give me £40? 50, 60, 70 and sold to the Ladies Slimming Club.

The next item has been donated by Captain Horatio Smith and is a collection of telescopes and binoculars. And I have £40, 50, no more? Sold to the gentleman at the back. Can I have your bidding number please, 20-20, how appropriate.

Now, we must thank the local Building Supply Company for a quantity of scaffolding planks, poles and fittings. I have a commission bid of £45. If there is no further interest – sold to the Young Wives Leisure Group.

Our next lot consists of 6 gents designer suits and has been handed in by Mrs Duff, who is with us this evening. I can start the bidding at £200 from Mr Duff, 300, 400, 500. Mrs Duff, you do realise you're bidding on your own item? Oh, you want your husband to have to pay to get his suits back. I see. Yes, Mr Duff, we have checked to see that all the suits are intact, no missing sleeves. £1000 from Mr Duff to regain his own property. Sold.

Next, a not unrelated item from Miss Erotica from those discreet premises next to the undertaker. Yes, Mrs Duff, we all know about your husband's connection with 69 High

Street but I don't feel we need the details just at this point. Perhaps later? Miss Erotica has donated some fur lined handcuffs and a selection of chains and padlocks. Can I ask for £20? 30, 40, 50, 60, 70, £80. Sold to the gentleman near the door. Thank you, Vicar.

And that concludes our charity auction. This year's chosen good cause is the home for retired auctioneers. Many thanks.

Small Talk

Hello, nice to see you again, Mrs Fairley-Bright. Oh, sorry, Mrs Bright-Fairley. I keep making that mistake, don't I? But tell me, have you always been hyphenated or is it a recent affliction? Oh, well it's very fashionable to renew one's vows on the first anniversary but not so common to file for divorce on the second one, but you were probably wise to keep the name for the sake of the twins. As I said, nice to see you again but I've just spotted Elspeth over in the corner – bye for now.

Elspeth, dear, I haven't seen you for months. I do like that top you're wearing. Tesco? Really? But it looks quite new so why are you calling it 'this old thing'? Well I don't consider something from last summer as being old, but then a lot of my wardrobe dates back to the last century, as I always go for quality rather than quantity. And I didn't even realise Tesco sold clothes!

Mrs Moncrieffe, how are you these days? I hear you've managed to sell your house at last. These ex-local authority properties are always such an unknown quantity on the resale market, although you had done a lot to it. Did the stone cladding and the hot tub on the patio help the sale, do you think? So where are you moving to? You're converting a windmill? How completely splendid. It'll be an absolute nightmare getting things to fit around it but I'm sure you've thought of that and at least your circular bed will fit.

Of course, our house is a conversion too. No, not a station or a barn – they're so common these days. Our former toilet block is just so unique. Yes, it is a bit 'inconvenient' having to put 20p in the bathroom door in the middle of the night but it's such a feature and the cash really mounts up, especially with George's bladder problems but let's not go into that now. And it only took a couple of years for the locals to stop trying to break through the front door on their way home from the pub. The stains on the porch were really quite easy to remove – a quick trip with the Marigolds and some disinfectant and they hardly show at all now, although the camellias sadly died despite the garden centre saying they liked acid soil!

Margaret! Coo-ee! Over here! How are you keeping dear? Jessie was telling me just last week that you've had heart trouble and split from your partner and all because of the BBC. It's all true? How devastating for you. What did Dr Jackson say about it? Well, with the best will in the world, Margaret, I can't see how taking up Scrabble is going to help. I know you don't need a partner for it but I'm still in the dark here. Oh, Margaret, how was I supposed to know Jessie was talking about the Beginners' Bridge Club and if hearts were the only suit you could recognise I'm not surprised your partner refused to play with you anymore. Perhaps Scrabble would be a better choice after all. You have a good working knowledge of the alphabet and you'll always have you Rs to fall back on! That was a joke dear – just forget I said it.

Wait 'til I get hold of Jessie – misleading me like that. No, she couldn't manage this afternoon. Said she had to wait in for the window cleaner – again. Really, it's so un-subtle. He's there every week, never takes his ladders off his van and doesn't even give the patio doors a cursory wipe. She thinks none of us realise what he's doing with his squeegee. Well I must be off now. I want to catch the window cleaner as he leaves Jessie's to see if he can give my Velux a quick rub down.

The Three Moons

Isn't this exciting, George? This holiday sounds unlike anything we've ever done before, and so reasonably priced. Now then, let's get the postcode for 'The Three Moons' into the satnag. There must be a postcode, George, everywhere has a postcode. Well, okay, just type in the hotel name and see what happens. Oh, my goodness, it's never done that before! That glow is a very unpleasant shade of green, and it seems to be vibrating. Ah, it's settled down now so let's be off. That's not the usual voice – it's like a cross between Margaret Thatcher and Graham Norton. Have you been fiddling with the settings again? All right, machine, we're going and yes, we'll take the second exit on the roundabout, no need to keep on about it.

Right then, what next? George, did I hear wrongly or did it just say to follow this road for 3.4 light years? That can't be correct, but we'll keep heading this way and see what happens. It may reset itself or perhaps I need a hearing test. Is that a patch of fog ahead or is someone having a bonfire? It's very thick, whatever it is and it's getting very cold now. I'll crank up the heating to fan assisted Regulo 9. At least the traffic is very light – almost non-existent actually – we haven't passed anything for ages – but the fog has turned distinctly purple, or is that my eyes? Remind me to visit the optician when we get home.

To quote Emily, 'do you think we're nearly there yet'? I'm gasping for a cuppa. Oh, look, yes, there it is on the left – 'Welcome to The Three Moons'. It looks lovely, let's hope we can find a handy parking space as I don't fancy lugging the cases for miles. Well done, George, beautifully parked and right beside the door, and there's a very handsome young man coming to meet us.

Thank you so much, young man. Of course we'll call you Sebastian. Yes, our luggage is in the boot. What's that? A cup of tea in the lounge sounds delightful – you must have read my mind. Isn't this lovely, George? A spectacular view of the three moons, a pink one, a green one and a yellow one and set off by a delicate lilac sky – I wonder how they do that? Probably with computers. Excellent tea, too, with dainty sandwiches, although I did think it a bit strange when the waitress asked what time I'd like my hearing and sight tests!

Have you noticed how incredibly attractive all the staff are? I see you have, but just remember your age, dear, and try not to drool. Here comes that receptionist again. George! Where do you think you're going? Come back here at once. Well, really, one word from me and he does as he likes. Forty years of training down the drain.

I really am feeling rather uncomfortable in this place. The staff all seem to be able to read minds. In fact, I think I want to go home. I'd head back to the car if only I had the keys. Hello again, Sebastian. Oh, you have our car keys – excellent. I expect George dropped them in his haste to follow that young girl.

Now then, where is the car? I thought we'd parked nearer the door than this, but never mind. I'll just set the satnag for 'home' and while it's computing that I have a couple of things I need to think about. First of all, how on earth can I describe this place on Trip Adviser and secondly, if I think really hard about Sebastian, could I take him home with me in place of George?

Here be Dragons

The Sewing, Knitting and Craft Group met on
   Wednesday each week.
The group was very popular, the reason not hard to seek.
Mrs Johnston always started off, 'Did you hear about
   young May?
She's been staying out late at night and is now in the
   family way!'
Irene Higgins spoke up next with news of Mrs O'Hare
Who hadn't been seen around for days since the news of
   her husband's affair.
They discussed the implications of Janet Mason's twins,
Jimmy Wilson's shop-lifting, and other local sins.
It was rumoured that the Postmistress was seriously in
   debt.
This was due in no small part to Bingo on the net!
Throughout all this they knitted or went on with their
   sewing.
The blankets and the quilting grew as the gossip kept on
   flowing.
And so the well-attended group that ran without a hitch
Had recently thought to change its name to The Ladies
   Stitch 'n' Bitch.

What's in a Name?

Hello, Emily, Granny here. So Mummy's letting you answer the phone today? Oh, she's "up to her elbows in poo". And how are your baby brothers today? Do they have names yet? Excellent – what have you decided? Yes, I know you were very disappointed they couldn't be Sven and Olaf from 'Frozen' but those names don't really go with your surname. In years to come they'll thank you for not insisting on your choices. Trust Granny on that one.

So, last I heard Daddy wanted Jeffrey and Jeremy but Mummy preferred Thomas and Tobias if she couldn't have Pasha and Aljaz from "Strictly". I'm very relieved your Daddy put his foot down on that one, Emily. Pasha and Aljaz would have been even worse that Sven and Olaf when the boys started school. So what happened, Emily? Ah, they 'compermised' with one choice each. Jeffrey and Tobias. That's a relief. I don't know if I'd ever have been at ease with two grandsons called Tom and Jerry!

Snow

Oh look, George, it's been snowing overnight. Doesn't the garden look pretty? It's the only time our garden looks as nice as everyone else's. I do like snow! Of course it was forecast but I'm sure they said to expect about twenty-five centimetres at lower levels and that looks more like ten inches to me but then they're always getting it wrong. Let's have breakfast then we can see about getting the path cleared before the postman's due.

Right George, I'll need to hunt at the back of the cupboard for my snow boots. You can try to reach the shed and unearth the snow scoop. Every winter we say we should have brought it nearer the door whenever snow is forecast, but we never do. Why don't you put on your golfing waterproofs to keep your ankles dry? Well, if they're in the shed too that's not much help. Never mind, I'll lay out a change of socks for you on the radiator for when we're finished. Don't say I'm not good to you. Off you go.

I finally located my boots underneath the cushions for the sun-lounger, so that's me all kitted out. Now if you start at the gate and work backwards I'll begin at the door and we'll meet in the middle. Well, your ankles are already damp so there's no point in me getting wet too – these boots are shorter that I remembered them.

No, dear, don't put the snow there – you'll squash the snowdrops; they're very good at pushing up through snow but I feel that a mountain of slush may be beyond their capabilities, especially if this snowy wonderland hangs around for a while. Yes, that'll do fine, dump it all on the lawn. It's not much further for you to carry it, really it isn't, and the extra exercise will do you good.

Do you remember that time when the children were small when we made two snowmen on the bollards in the lane? We really laughed when that delivery driver couldn't see it was a footpath and tried to mow down the snowmen to get through. I often wonder how he explained the dents to his boss. Yes, I've always liked snow.

That's us finished – that didn't take long, did it? A nice clear path. Now, when you were in the darkest depths of the shed did you come across that white tub of grit I got when it was reduced at the end of last winter? Well if it really is as inaccessible as you claim we'll just have to give it a light sprinkle with table salt and hope it doesn't freeze. Oh dear, the snow seems to be starting again. I do hope all that work isn't going to be wasted. You know, George, I've never liked snow!

The Canal Festival

Good afternoon everyone and welcome. Let's get this last meeting before our Canal Festival underway. As you know, this is the second of what we hope will become an annual event. Last year's inaugural festival was successful but there were, inevitably, things that could have gone better and we hope to be more prepared for the unexpected this year.

With this in mind, Eric, just a word about your canal-side nature walks. Please be sure to remind your groups not to stray from the towpath, particularly on the side nearest the canal as the banks are somewhat unstable in places, and should there be a repeat of last year's unfortunate incident involving the doctor's wife, I would hope you would deal with it in a more diplomatic manner and refrain from shouting, "for God's sake, woman, stop screeching and just stand up. The water's only two feet deep."

Now then, Margaret, you're once again in charge of the tea tent, which, by the way, is a sturdier model this year although the weather forecast is quite promising and last year's freak tornado was surely a one-off. Although the little jars of wild flowers on the tables are undoubtedly pretty, they did attract insects and the pollen caused some visitors, namely Mrs Oliver, to sneeze rather violently. Nevertheless, I do not feel we should have been held accountable for the loss of her teeth when she sneezed them into the canal. Similarly with Mr Jamieson's spectacles which fell overboard as he leaned out of the barge in a futile attempt to pat a passing duck. Robert has managed to persuade the local diving club to be on hand just in case there are any similar incidents this year.

Following on from there, Janet, is the public liability insurance in place? Excellent. I expect the premium went up a bit after last year? HOW MUCH? Well really, surely there weren't all that many people who got wet enough to sue. We kept it to single figures – not counting the dogs.

One last point. James, have you printed up the posters? Excellent. We'll get them distributed this weekend. Hold one up so we can get a look at it. A triumph of clip-art if I may say so. Er, James, isn't the festival on the 24th, not the 25th as it says on all 100 of those posters? Yes, it might be a good idea to re-do them. We don't want everyone turning up a day late, do we?

Well, that's everything on the agenda. See you all at the festival and remember our motto – Let's Stay Dry!

Little Weeds

Right then, George, I bought some weed-killer when I was out so we can deal with the lawn now – it really is looking dreadful. I suspect there are almost as many weeds as grass. I didn't want the kind of weed-killer that comes as granules and they didn't have a ready mixed spray in the quantity we need so I had to get the kind you dilute yourself. Now what are we going to mix it up in? Our red watering-can disintegrated after you 'accidentally' strimmed it. We'll have to use one of the green ones. Either we'll, sorry, you'll have to wash it out thoroughly afterwards or we could paint a big 'W' on the side. W for weed-killer, George, what else could I mean? Oh, I suppose you do have a point there, it could just as easily be W for water. That is rather a fundamental flaw with the plan. Back to washing it out then.

I suppose I'd better – reluctantly – read the instructions although it does go against all my instincts. Oh, look at what it says on the label – FOR USE AS AN AMATEUR LAWN WEED-KILLER. Did you know there were professional lawns? Neither did I. Professional probably refers to bowling greens or playing fields or even that striped effect Mr Thomas in the Crescent has, but it is rather humbling to realise your lawn is considered amateur.

Right, what's next? George, how much is 15ml? I find it so much easier to cope with measuring by the teaspoonful. I do know the watering-can holds two gallons but the instructions are in litres. I told you there was no point in my reading them. Never mind, I'll just add a good glug plus a drip or two for luck and hope for the best. What's the worst that can happen? It's supposed to work in 24 hours, so by tomorrow morning we'll have a lovely weed free lawn. Won't that be nice? Yes, it will, George.

Isn't this exciting? When I open the blinds we'll have a beautiful green lawn without a weed in sight, even if it is classed as amateur. Ready, George? Oh, my goodness. Just look at that. I can't believe it. How on earth did that happen? It's just an expanse of shrivelled brown-ness with no sign of a single blade of green-ness. There must have been a higher proportion of weed to grass than I realised. Perhaps my somewhat random approach to making up the solution didn't help either. Please note, George, I said that before you could. I'm reluctantly taking full responsibility for 'lawn gate'.

But now the question is what to do about it? Re-seeding will take forever and we'll need to keep Emily and the boys off it for months – yes I know the boys aren't even crawling yet but they soon will be. I much prefer the idea of children running amok outside rather than inside. The same problem arises with turfing it – you can't walk on it for ages, let alone allow children to play on it and it needs regular watering or it shrinks and looks like an outdoor patchwork quilt.

Slabs are a non-starter for safety reasons. Emily is amazingly accident prone and she'd be bound to fall and break something if only to spite us. It's too big an area to slab anyway and the same goes for gravel – it'd look like an inaccessible car park.

I think we already have enough decking and the maintenance level is quite high after a year or two. No, George, you may not have a power washer. You cause quite enough trouble with an ordinary hose. Mrs Hetherington still crosses the road rather than pass by our fence after you accidentally – you say – sprayed her with Miracle-gro as she was out for an evening stroll. Being only 4 feet 10 she took your growing comments very personally.

No, I think the only solution is going to be artificial turf. It's really nice to look at and walk on, honestly, it is. Well, I did just happen to price it a week or so ago when I was in the garden centre. Wasn't that a happy coincidence? The company does all the prep work for you and lay it all – there's even a choice of greens. What could be better? You'd never have to cut the lawn again and we could sell the lawnmower, giving you more space in the shed for you 'hobby'. (Auntie still hasn't quite recovered, you know).

So, that's it settled. We'll get the experts in to give us a beautiful, no maintenance plastic lawn. I wonder if that will count as professional?

That was Very Strange

Right, George, your tea's in the oven; it'll be ready in half an hour. Joyce will be here any minute to collect me for our sponsored silence. Are you smirking? Of course I'll find it difficult, if not impossible – that's why I managed to get so much sponsorship. I've reached £12 per minute because everyone knows I'm inclined to talk a fair bit. There's the doorbell. I'll be off then and I'll be back about 10 o'clock. Bye.

George, wake up, it's not bedtime yet. Just wait 'til you hear what I've been up to. Of course it was all Joyce's fault. Somewhere along the line she got her wires crossed and what she thought was a sponsored silence was actually a sponsored séance. Even before we discovered the mistake Joyce had already had a 'moment' at the door of the Town Hall when we met Irene who said the meeting was in the Topliss Room. Irene had to physically restrain Joyce from bolting while I explained it was T-O-P-L-I-S-S after some long dead councillor and no disrobing was required.

So we went into the Topliss Room to find it lit by one 40watt bulb and swathed in miles of velvet and other materials that reminded me of your Mother's old curtains and Irene dropped the bombshell that we were to participate in a séance for charity. There were about a dozen of us and we were all directed to sit around a big table where we could hold hands and we waited for 'Mystic Morag' whose grand entrance would have been more impressive if she a) hadn't been a poorly disguised Nellie from the fruit and veg counter in the Co-op and b) hadn't tripped over her flowing robes and sworn in a most un-mystical fashion.

But anyway, we all held hands while Nellie – sorry, Morag – started to chant and appeared to go into some kind of trance. Irene had explained to us that we would earn sponsorship based on how many of the spirits Morag contacted we were able to claim a relationship with. I hope you have your chequebook ready, George, as you know how many dead relatives I have, all of them just as likely to be talkative in the afterlife as they were in this one.

Well, the next hour was amongst the strangest of my life. Every time Mystic Mo heard a voice, she would ask us if anyone knew a James or Ethel or Fred and if you were able to claim kinship you were awarded one spirit on you sponsorship form. At one time the names were coming so quickly that it was like a game of mystical bingo as we all tried to claim dead relations. I'm sure I heard Joyce shout 'house' at one point. I had to toss a coin with Mrs Edgar as we both had a grandfather named Thomas, but no-one was prepared to lay claim to an Auntie Margery, so Morag had to move on. In total I claimed 10 spirits so that'll be a well-earned £120 for the Save Our Swamp project.

But, George, the strangeness wasn't over. Of course, we all accepted that it was just a bit of fun and Nellie wasn't a real mystic, but as we were about to leave the draperies moved as if in a draught even although the door and windows were all closed then the 40watt bulb flickered and went out. We made 'light' of it and laughed but Nellie turned ever so pale and slumped in a heap on the floor. As our Brownie first aid hadn't covered fainting, we left Irene to sort her out and slipped out as unobtrusively as possible.

It was such a strange evening, but the whole thing was just fun after all. George, is there a window open in here? It's turned a bit chilly and now our lights are flickering. How strange. I suppose it really was rubbish, wasn't it, George?

The Five Senses of Christmas

Right then, George, we've done everything Delia suggested for a perfect Christmas lunch. This is 'resting' time – no, not you, it's the turkey that's resting. You can't be tired after peeling a few potatoes and carrots. So let's get this culinary extravaganza on to the plates. Doesn't it look amazing? Delia never lets you down. Almost a shame to hack into it but I really am very hungry so let's get going.

Yes, thank you, I'll have my annual sprout. I'm hoping the cranberry sauce will disguise the taste. Because it's Christmas, George, that's why I always eat one sprout even although I violently dislike them. Mash next and a couple of roasties. It smells delicious but there is just a tinge of something else. I know – it's that Christmas aftershave Auntie gave you. I thought when you un-wrapped it that 'cranberry 'n' clove' were an odd combination. Perhaps you should have drunk it instead of wearing it. Cloves always remind me of the dentist. Dear Auntie, she always chooses such original gifts. I'm looking forward to using the unusual combination of matching wellingtons and toilet brush holder. I remember for my 17th birthday she gave me a pickle fork, saying that she thought it would come in handy when I started learning to drive! And she gave us an electric carving knife for a wedding present when the nearest we could afford to a joint of meat was a tin of Spam.

Well, that was quite delicious. Thanks, Delia. I'll just go and deal with the mini puddings and custard. Oh, there's the phone. That'll be Joyce. I must remember to thank her for the bottle of port, even if we did give it to them two years ago. Could you do something with the dessert please? Thanks, I won't be long.

Hello, Joyce. Yes, Happy Christmas to you, too. We're between courses so I can't chat for long as I've left George in the kitchen. Thank you so much for the port. We really appreciate the thought. Oh, my goodness, can you hear that noise? It's the smoke alarm – I'd better go. I can see George doing the dance of the seven veils in the hall, flapping ineffectively with a tea towel. Bye for now, Joyce, I'll speak to you again in a couple of days.

George, just open the back door and the alarm will stop. That's better, blessed silence. Now, what happened? The handle of the custard pot seems to be smouldering gently and it won't stop while it's still over a lit burner. No – turn off the burner, DON'T lift the pot. Quickly, hold your hand under the cold tap – that'll help and while I realise you're in pain, bad language contributes nothing to the situation. Of course I'm sure the cold water is what's needed – I may have failed my Brownie first aid badge but I can still make a sling from a triangular bandage if I was ever required to do so and I distinctly recall that cold water is the way to treat minor burns.

Now then, can these puddings be rescued? I bought them at the school Xmas Fayre, made by the 3rd year cookery class. I do hope they used a Delia recipe. The custard will be okay if I don't scrape the bottom of the pot. No, George, it isn't burnt – it's caramelised. That's the how cookery shows describe burnt, so we will too. You know, I hate to have to admit you're right, but the custard's burnt, and the mini puddings have a strange woolly texture. But never mind, the rest of the meal was just lovely. Gosh, I do feel full, but it is Christmas after all.

WELL REALLY

A Dream Holiday in Limerick

The duo of Thelma and Carol
Were sightseeing up in Balmoral,
When H.M. the Queen
Jumped out from between
A lavender bush and a laurel.

Off cycled Harvey and Andy
Southwards towards Tonypandy
As the miles flew by
They got tired and dry
So popped into a pub for a shandy.

That adventurous pair, Ralph and Anne
Went on a dream trip to Japan.
Anne loved the raw fish
Said it was quite delish
But Ralph had his fried in a pan.

A scholarly gent name of Iain
Flew off to the blue Caribbean.
He lay on the sand
With a book in each hand
Plus Robin, his antipodean.

Poor Olwen could not enjoy Rome
As she'd left some essentials at home.
It's hard to relax
And take in tourist facts
Without underwear, glasses or phone.

Will and Doreen set off to explore
French battlefields from days of yore,
But they didn't get far
For a broken down car
Meant their holiday plans were no more

And Lynda her Bill did embarrass
When they went for a weekend to Paris.
She stepped off a bateau
And tripped on a gateau
Coming down with a bump on her …….bottom.

Acknowledgements

Thanks to my nephew, Hamish, for finding time to do the sketch for the cover.

Porthmadog U3A creative Writing group have given me continual encouragement and advice and without them this book would never have come to fruition. Thank you all.

Finally, thanks to my husband, the 'long suffering' Bill, who is nothing like 'George' and who must be heartily sick of anything remotely resembling a monologue.

About The Seagull Trust

Founded in 1978 the *Seagull Trust Cruises* charity offers cruises on Scotland's canals for people with special needs. From small beginnings, Seagull Trust Cruises hosted 22,841 passengers on 2444 cruises in 2016.

A completely voluntary charity, cruises run from branches at Ratho near Edinburgh, Falkirk, Kirkintilloch and Highland near Inverness.